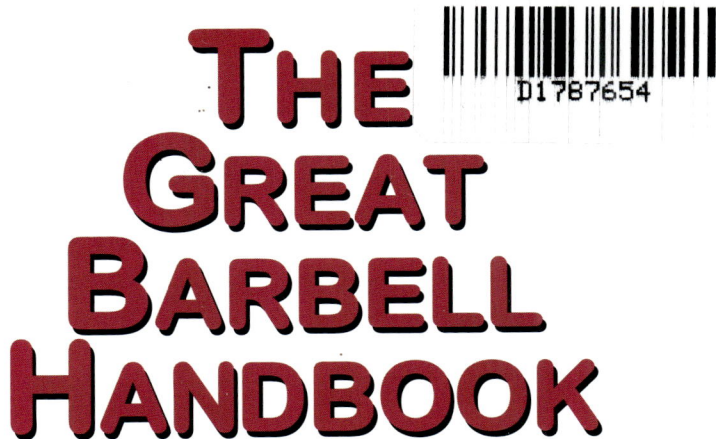

THE GREAT BARBELL HANDBOOK

WRITTEN BY

Bill Luke

EDITED BY

EXPERT: STRENGTH TRAINING & GENERAL FITNESS
Andre Noel Potvin
    M.SC., C.S.C.S., CES

EXPERT: STRENGTH AND CONDITIONING & FITNESS
Bill Luke
    Ph.D., C.S.C.S., Registered Kinesiologist

EXPERT: STRETCHING & GENERAL FITNESS
Nikos Apostolopoulos
    BPHE, NCCP-L3, AACA, AAA, ACSM, IASP

GENERAL EDITOR
Michael Jespersen

COPY EDITOR
Karl Thorson

First Printing

Copyright © 2003
by Productive Fitness Products Inc.

Consult your physician before starting any exercise program. This is of particular importance if you are over 35 and have been inactive for a period of time. The author and publisher disclaim any liability from loss, injury, or damage, personal or otherwise, resulting from the procedures in this book.

We would like to thank Heavenly Bodies for supplying women's clothing:

www.heavenlybodiessport.com

Published 2003
Productive Fitness Products Inc.
2289-135A St.
Surrey, B.C. V4A 9V2

For quantity discounts please call toll free:
1-888-221-8833
or write:
Productive Fitness Products Inc.
P.O. Box 2325
Blaine, WA 98231-2325
or e-mail
 mike@productivefitness.com

Visit our Website: www.productivefitness.com

Luke, Bill, 1953-
  The great barbell handbook: the quick reference guide to barbell exercises/Bill Luke, Andre Noel Potvin

  ISBN 0-9731262-1-3
  1. Barbells--Handbooks, manuals, etc. 2. Weight training--Handbooks, manuals, etc. I. Potvin, Andre Noel, 1961- II. Title.
  GV547.3.L84 2003   613.7'13   C2003-910622-5

TABLE OF CONTENTS

Introduction	4
Weight Training Safety Tips	5
Body Diagrams	6-7
What You'll Need	8-10
Accessories	11
Exercise Techniques	12-13
How To Set Up A Program	14-16
Staying Motivated	17
Stretching	18-22

Barbell Exercises

Shoulders
Front Press—Seated	23
Military Press	24
Upright Row	25
Front Raise	26
Shrug	27
Push Press	28

Chest
Bench Press	29
Bench Press—Narrow Grip	30
Incline Bench Press	31
Pullover	32

Back
Bent-Over Row	33
T-Bar Row—Two Arm	34
T-Bar Row—One Arm	35

Biceps
Standing Bicep Curl	36
Bicep Curl—E-Z Kurl Bar	37
Seated Isolation Curl	38
Preacher Curl	39

Triceps
Lying Triceps Extension	40
Seated Triceps Extension	41
Standing Overhead Triceps Extension	
E-Z Kurl Bar (Narrow Grip)	42
Tricep Bar (Neutral Grip)	42
Barbell Kickback	43
Reverse Grip Bench Press	44

Forearms
Reverse Curl—Straight Bar	45
Reverse Curl—E-Z Kurl Bar	45
Wrist Curl—Bench	46
Reverse Wrist Curl—Bench	47
Wrist Curl—Thighs	48
Reverse Wrist Curl—Thighs	49
Behind-The-Back Wrist Curl	50

Legs
Front Squat	51
High Bar Back Squat	52-53
Power Squat	54
Split Squat	55
Lunge	56
Side Lunge	57
Step Up	58
Conventional Deadlift	59
Sumo Deadlift	60

Calves
Seated Calf Raise	61

Other Products	62-64

INTRODUCTION

Whether you are a novice to strength training or have been training with dumbbells and want a little more variety or challenge, then barbell training is an excellent option.

In this book we try to take a functional approach to strength training, which simply means that the exercises you see here resemble movements done in everyday life. The idea is that if you can get strong and efficient at these movements, then the everyday tasks you demand from your body get easier and easier. In addition, with increased strength comes a sense of self-assurance and confidence.

Given today's hectic life, setting up a complete gym at home is a practical and time-saving alternative to the gym. By adding barbells to your setup, you have brought yourself closer to the variety of exercises that are available in most gyms and health clubs. Safety is an important concern when at home, and you should ideally have a spotter when performing most of the exercises. While it is not always practical to have a spotter at the ready, take the necessary steps to make sure the exercises can be done safely.

While all the equipment you see in this book is not necessary for a good workout, many of the items will make your workout more pleasant. Equipment makes all the difference from both a performance, and a safety standpoint.

Good training.

Weight Training
SAFETY TIPS

✔ **Always warm up before you start a workout.** Try to do a total-body warm-up before you start training. A good example of a total-body warm-up is using a rowing or skiing machine. It is especially important to warm up the specific muscle groups you are going to be using. A warm-up can be as simple as performing the specific exercise at 25% to 50% of the weight you normally lift for a high number of repetitions.

✔ **Use proper posture.** Maintaining proper posture will greatly reduce chances of injury and maximize exercise benefit. When standing, always keep your feet shoulder-width apart. Do not lock your knees; it puts an unnecessary strain on them. Keep your back flat and straight, abdominal muscles contracted, and make sure not to twist or arch your back in order to complete an exercise.

✔ **Use proper form.** Focus on only working the muscle groups intended for the exercise you are doing. If you feel strain elsewhere, you may need someone to critique your exercise motion or reevaluate the amount of weight you are lifting. Keeping proper form also means lifting in a smooth, fluid motion. Know when your muscles are too tired to keep going.

✔ **Breathe properly.** Never hold your breath during any part of an exercise. Holding your breath may cause severe intra-thoracic pressure and raise blood pressure, leading to dizziness, blackout or worse! The rule of thumb is to exhale slowly on exertion and inhale on the return part of the exercise.

Exception: In some cases experienced weight training athletes may hold their breath to support the spine. Breath holding plus contracted abdominals can increase the stability of the vertebral column and help maintain a "flat back". This breath holding should be for a maximum of 1-2 seconds— any longer can result in dizziness, lightheadedness, increased blood pressure and disorientation, and fainting.

✔ **Stop training if you feel pain.** If you feel pain during a specific exercise, stop immediately. Any continuation may aggravate an existing injury. Reevaluate your routine to make sure you are doing a proper warm-up. Decrease the amount of weight you are lifting.

Body
DIAGRAMS

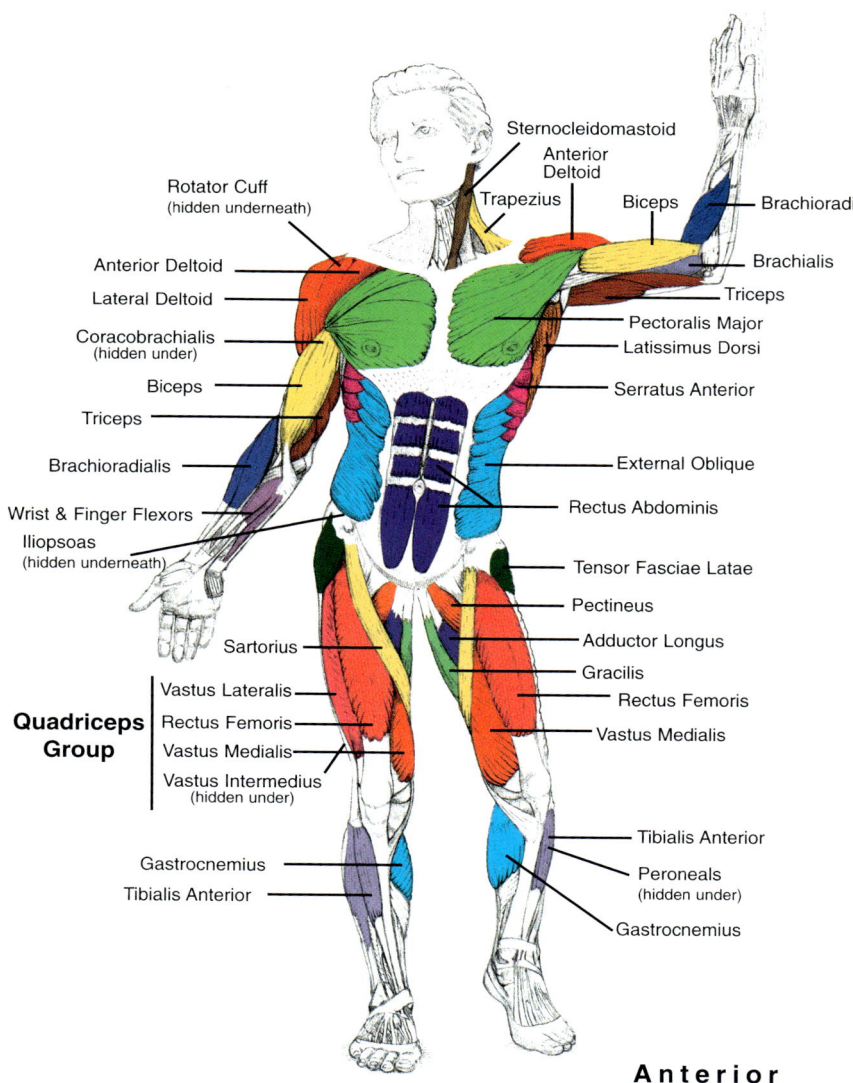

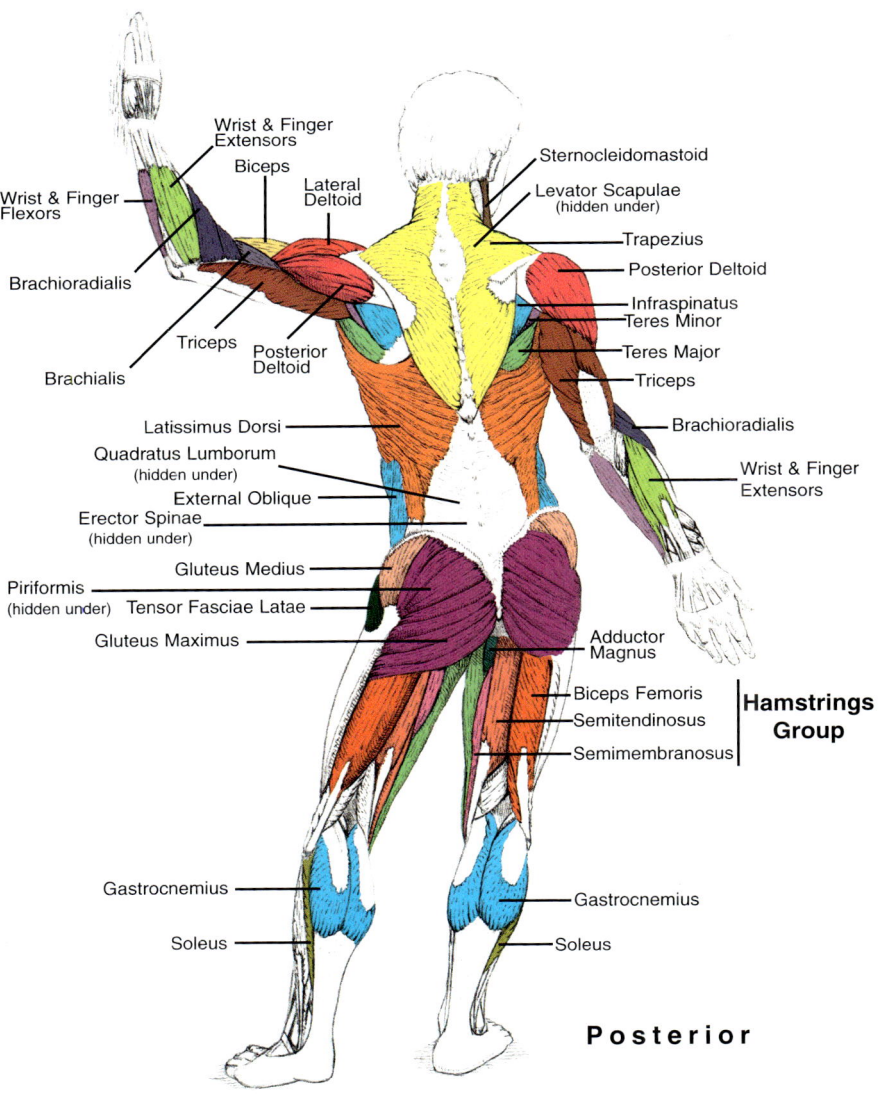

WHAT YOU'LL NEED

STANDARD BARS

The standard barbell comes in lengths of 4-7 feet and requires weight plates with a 1-inch-diameter center hole. Metal or vinyl-covered plates for the standard weight lifting bar range from 1.25 to 35 pounds. In the home setting, it is typical to have adjustable bars, while in most commercial gyms, the bar weight is fixed and increases in 5 to 10 pound increments.

OLYMPIC BARS

In most commercial settings you will see heavier "Olympic" bars in lengths of 5, 6 or 7 feet. Olympic bars require plates that have a 2-inch-diameter hole. Olympic bars are accurately manufactured and used in competitive weight lifting events and when heavy loads are used in certain exercises, such as the bench press and squat. Plates for Olympic bars range from 2.5 to 45 pounds.

TRICEP BAR

The tricep bar allows for exercises with the neutral grip (knuckles facing out) and is used by more experienced weight trainers who want to "hit" the tricep muscles from different angles. The bar comes in standard design and Olympic specifications.

E-Z KURL BAR

The E-Z Kurl bar is a specialized bar that permits the biceps and triceps muscles to be trained at different angles than the straight bar would allow.

COLLARS

You should never use barbells without first having the weights securely fixed in place by collars. Collars prevent the plates from shifting or falling off the bar, both of which can lead to serious injury. The "spring-collar" is the easiest and fastest to use, although there are other "screw-in" varieties as well.

SQUAT RACK

Squat racks or a spotter should be used whenever squats are done. The rack should have adjustable bars that are set at the lowest depth you want to descend to. If for some reason the last repetition can't be completed, you can simply "sit down" and the squat rack catches the bar while you recover.

BENCH WITH WEIGHT RACK

The flat or incline bench with bar rack or a spotter should be used any time lying lifts are being completed. The weight support should be adjustable to permit individuals of different arm lengths to efficiently use the bench.

BAR PAD

Some individuals find that resting a bar on their upper back and shoulders is uncomfortable. The bar pad may add some relief, but it does move the bar away from the body a small amount, which can increase balance problems.

ADJUSTABLE FLAT TO INCLINE BENCH

A flat-to-incline bench is essential for doing a proper barbell workout because it allows you a more complete range of movement. The front seat should be adjustable upwards to prevent you from sliding off the bench when it is set at the incline position. When exercising, always set the backrest to an upright position to support your back if you are in a seated position. For instance, when performing an overhead shoulder press exercise, make sure the backrest is set in the vertical position. A good flat-to-incline bench should be easy to adjust and made of 10-11 gauge steel.

THE STEP

Using a Step, such as the one shown, will add a lot of functionality and variability to your exercises. Look for one with a good base of support and that has no lateral (side-to-side) movement. It is also good to be able to adjust the height.

ACCESSORIES

EXERCISE GLOVES

The two main reasons for using gloves are to protect your skin from becoming rough or calloused and to reduce the stress on finger joints. The leather padding of the gloves will protect your skin from the knurled grips of the barbells. Gloves will also help to dissipate the pull of the weight which may cause ligament damage to the delicate joints in your hand and fingers.

WEIGHT LIFTING BELT

Belts are not normally necessary when using barbells. Use of a weight belt may be appropriate for certain exercises such as the squat or other exercises that may increase stresses on the lower back.

CAUTION: Develop good abdominal and lower back muscular strength and concentrate on good technique even if using a weight belt.

There are generally two types of belts: leather and velcro. Leather belts can be uncomfortable and stiff until they are broken in, whereas velcro belts are comfortable immediately. Velcro belts can also be adjusted to your exact waist size, whereas the leather belts can only be adjusted to the next set of buckle holes.

STRAPS

Straps are used for lifting heavy barbells. The strap wraps around your wrist and comes out over the palm of your hand. You wrap the strap around the barbell until the weight is supported by your wrist and not your fingers. Straps can be effective when doing certain exercises such as the Bent-Over Row or Shoulder Shrugs.

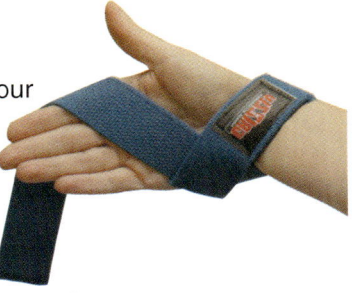

EXERCISE
TECHNIQUES

GRIPS

Different exercises will require different hand grips to ensure maximum efficiency and safety. There are two common grips (first two) used for most weighttraining exercises and two less common that are used when a strongergrip is needed.

1. Overhand grip
(pronated)- palms down,
thumbs under and knuckles up.

2. Underhand
(supinated)- palms up, thumbs over
and knuckles down.

3. Alternated grip —one underhand and one overhand grip (often used when heavier weights
are lifted).

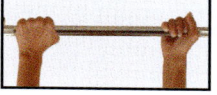

4. Hook grip—overhand grip with the thumb placed underneath the index and middle fingers.

*In all cases, the thumb is wrapped around the bar—this is called a **closed grip**. If the thumb is NOT wrapped around the bar it is called an **open grip** (not recommended as the bar is less stable with this grip).

GRIP WIDTH

Once the correct grip is selected, it is important to choose the most efficient "grip width"—this is the distance the hands are placed apart. Most exercises will require your hands to be shoulder-width apart, or close to it. The exact grip width is determined by the amount of weight being lifted and the focus of the exercise.

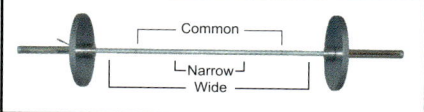

Exercise Techniques | 13

STABLE BODY POSITION

During all barbell exercises it is critical to maintain a stable body position. A stable body position keeps the body in proper alignment and thereby puts your back and joints in the strongest position for weight bearing and exercise performance. There are generally two approaches to establishing a stable body position:

    A. Setting the back—standing exercise
    B. 5-point contact—for exercises lying on a bench.

A. Setting the Back for Standing Barbell Exercises

1. Contract abdominal muscles.
2. Chest held up and out (helps prevent rounding).
3. Head in neutral position or slightly arched to prevent rounding of the back.
4. Flat or slightly arched back.

B. 5-Point Contact for Bench Exercises

1. Head touches bench.
2. Upper back and shoulders on bench.
3. Lower back on bench (or close to it).
4. Buttocks on bench.
5. Feet flat on the floor (use a foot lift if needed).

FOOT POSITION FOR STANDING EXERCISES

Most standing barbell exercises require feet parallel and slightly wider than shoulder-width apart. Feet should be flat on the floor with the back set.

EXERCISE RANGE OF MOTION

To ensure maximum strength and flexibility development without forfeiting technique or form, each exercise should be completed through the full range of motion (ROM). A slow and controlled motion in both the up and down phase is necessary for safety and efficiency.

* Some power exercises, for example, the Olympic lifts, are completed with maximum speed, but should still be under control to prevent excessive injury risk.

SPOTTER

A spotter can best be defined as someone that will gently assist you in completing a repetition when you are too fatigued to complete it alone. For standing exercises the spotter is also there to help should you lose your balance.

A WORD ON THE USE OF A SPOTTER

Any time you are trying maximum lifts or performing overhead or above-head exercises, safety must be considered. If a spotter is not available, use of a squat rack.

How To Set Up A
PROGRAM

1. ESTABLISH GOALS

Begin by setting specific and realistic goals. Ideally, set a long-term goal and then set a series of short-term goals that move you toward reaching your long-term goal. Once you have made the commitment to see your goal through, list exactly how you will attain this specific goal, including the number of workouts/week, type of activity, time of day for workout, and how you will incorporate this into your weekly schedule. For instance, if you want to increase your overall strength by 50%, record your beginning and your most recent level of strength.

<u>Week 1</u>
Bench press: 12 reps @ 15lbs
<u>Week 12</u>
Bench press: 12 reps @ 20lbs

Simply divide the most recent figure into the beginning figure and subtract 1 to get the percentage increase in strength.

1) 20lbs ÷ 15lbs = 1.33
2) 1.33 - 1 = .33 or 33%

Your increase in strength is 33%.

> **REPETITION, SET, AND WORKLOAD**
> A <u>Repetition</u> is a complete exercise movement from start to finish. One complete series of continuous, consecutive repetitions is called a <u>Set</u>. <u>Workload</u> refers to the amount of weight used in working a particular muscle or muscle group.

Look to see what changes in your lifestyle you will have to make to accommodate the new program. From both a motivational and safety perspective, it is a good idea to track your progress each and every time you work out. A training diary can help keep your workouts consistent and efficient.

2. COMPONENTS OF A GOOD STRENGTH TRAINING PROGRAM

Frequency
Exercise each muscle group 2-4 times per week. Allow a minimum of 48 hours rest for each muscle group worked. If you are doing a total-body workout, three training sessions per week, performed on every second day, is adequate.

Duration
A workout session should take anywhere from 30 minutes to 1 hour to complete.

Range of Motion
Moving through a complete range of motion (ROM) allows the muscle to stretch before contraction and increases the number of fibers being recruited. This produces maximum contraction and force. By working the full ROM, while maintaining proper form and technique, flexibility will be maintained or even increased.

Speed of Movement
Strength training movements should be slow and controlled. Do not use momentum to complete an exercise. Momentum puts unnecessary stress on tendons, ligaments, and joints and does not develop increased strength.

Proper Form
Focus on the proper motion of the exercise while concentrating on the specific muscles being used. Do not sacrifice proper form to lift heavier weight or to perform more repetitions.

Rest Interval
Allow a brief pause between sets to give the muscles a chance to partially recover before working them again. For hypertrophy or muscle size development allow 1 to 1.5 minutes; for endurance allow 30 to 60 seconds; and for strength allow 3-5 minutes.

3. EXERCISE ORDER
When designing a strength training routine, always try to work the larger muscle groups first. Exercises that involve more than one muscle group (compound exercises) should be at the beginning of the routine, and exercises that involve only one muscle group (isolation exercises) should follow. This will prevent your muscles from becoming prematurely tired and interfering with correct form on more complex exercises.

Order of Muscle Groups by size for:
        1) Upper Body
        2) Lower Body
        3) Core.

* For a full-body workout you can alternate upper body and lower body exercises to save on recovery time between sets.

Upper Body
- Chest (pectoralis major and pectoralis minor)
- Upper back (latissimus dorsi, upper and middle trapezius, and rhomboids)
- Shoulders (anterior, medial, and posterior deltoids and upper trapezius)
- Rotator cuff (supraspinatus, infraspinatus, teres minor, and subscapularis)
- Triceps (long, middle, and short heads)
- Biceps (biceps brachii, brachialis, brachioradialis)
- Forearms (flexors and extensors)

Lower Body
- Gluteal muscle group (buttocks)
- Hip muscle group (psoas, adductors, and abductors)
- Quadriceps muscle group (vastus medialis, vastus lateralis, vastus intermedius, and rectus femoris)
- Hamstrings muscle group (semimembranosus, semitendinosus, and biceps femoris)
- Calf muscle group (soleus, gastrocnemius, anterior tibialis)

Core (Core Group of Muscles)
- Abdominals (transverse, rectus abdominis, and obliques)
- Lower back (quadratus lumborum and erector spinae)

4. DESIGN YOUR PROGRAM

Go through each of the body sections in the exercise description section and pick out one to two exercises per body part. Write these exercises in your training diary or on a piece of paper. Mark next to each exercise the number of repetitions and sets you want to do and the workload or amount of weight to be lifted.

SAMPLE ROUTINE

If you are a beginner, a three-week pre-routine schedule is recommended. For the first week simply perform the exercises with very light weights. This will help you to develop proper form. Coordination is developed in the second and third weeks as you add a few pounds to each exercise. Once the three weeks have ended, begin adding more weight each week until you are barely capable of performing the required number of repetitions while maintaining correct form. The desired objective is to lift as much weight as possible, in a controlled movement, for the appropriate number of repetitions. In other words, challenge your body by increasing the workload as the exercises become easier.

EXERCISES	REPS	SETS	WORKLOAD*
Squat	8-12	3	moderate
Calf Raises	8-12	3	moderate
Bench Press	8-12	3	moderate
Bent-Over Row	8-12	3	moderate
Upright Row	8-12	3	moderate
Shoulder Press	8-12	3	moderate
Seated Triceps Extension	8-12	3	moderate
Bicep Curl	8-12	3	moderate
Wrist Curl	8-12	3	moderate
Reverse Wrist Curl	8-12	3	moderate
Abdominal Crunch	20-30	3	body weight

Staying Motivated

A. SET SHORT-TERM GOALS TO ACHIEVE LONG-TERM GOALS.
After setting long-term goals go back and break them up into smaller goals that are easier to achieve. Reward yourself each time you accomplish a goal.

B. MAKE A POINT OF HAVING FUN DURING YOUR WORKOUTS.
Get a training partner: someone who can offer support and encouragement when working out. Buy a walkman and exercise to your favorite music. Workouts are so much easier when they are fun.

C. ESTABLISH A DEFINITE TIME AND PLACE TO WORK OUT.
Force yourself to be consistent in your workouts for the first couple of months. This will help you to feel you are accomplishing your goals, it will set a pattern for future workouts, and it will help you to make exercise a part of your lifestyle.

D. KEEP A TRAINING JOURNAL TO MONITOR YOUR PROGRESS
If you're truly dedicated to getting the most out of your exercise routine you should consider keeping an accurate record of your weight training sessions. The whole benefit of doing any type of weight training comes in the form of progressive resistance. By gradually increasing either the weight lifted, the number of repetitions, or the number of sets, you challenge your body to perform a little better each time. The direct benefits of keeping a journal are: more organized routines, knowing how and when to challenge your body, reduced chance of injury by over-lifting, a sense of accomplishment from actually seeing your progress on paper.

STRETCHING

BY NIKOS APOSTOLOPOULOS, BPHE, NCCP-L3, AACA, AAA, ACSM, IASP

The two main purposes of stretching are prevention of injury caused by exercise or day-to-day activities and a faster rate of recovery from exercise. A regular stretching program will loosen muscle tissue, allowing an increased range of motion, which in turn helps prevent microtears at the muscle-tendon junction. Almost 90% of all injuries from muscle strain occur at the muscle-tendon junction, and repeated injury at this junction leads to a buildup of scar tissue, which impedes range of motion, adding stress on the joints. The sooner waste products from exercise (lactic acid) are removed from the muscle tissue, the sooner the muscle begins to heal. Stretching not only speeds removal of waste, but increases the muscle's ability to bring in more nutrients. Keeping the muscles and tendons loose results in an increased range of motion, which helps to maintain the integrity of the joints.

Benefits of regular stretching
- decreased risk of injury from exercise
- increased range of motion and overall flexibility
- increased rate of recovery from exercise
- increase in strength (studies have shown that after a muscle has been stretched it recruits more fibres to perform a given task.)
- faster removal of waste products

Nikos Apostolopoulos is the founder of Stretch Therapy®, and microStretching®. He is the director of the Serapis Stretch Therapy Clinic in Vancouver, British Columbia, Canada, the only clinic in the world pioneering the development of therapeutic stretching. The clinic uses Stretch Therapy and microStretching—recovery regeneration techniques based on functional clinical anatomy—to treat many professional, elite and amateur athletes and individuals suffering from various musculoskeletal disorders.

Nikos graduated from the Faculty of Physical and Health Education at the University of Toronto with an emphasis in Sports Medicine. He has over 20 years experience in gross and functional anatomy and is a member of the American Association of Anatomists (AAA), American Association of Clinical Anatomists (AACA), American College of Sports Medicine (ACSM), and the International Association for the Study of Pain. He is currently working on his book MicroStretching-A New Approach.

Principles of Stretching

Try to set up a daily stretch routine; adhering to a consistent stretch program can have a profound impact on how you feel on a day-to-day basis. Moreover, if you stretch on a daily basis you can forgo the required pre-workout stretch. Please note: a warm-up prior to exercise is still required.

The problem with some traditional stretches is the muscle you are trying to stretch is the same muscle used to provide stability and balance. You can't stretch a muscle that is already in use. You'll notice many of the following stretches involve a chair, bench, or wall to help isolate the target muscle group. By offering a base of support, you will completely relax the muscle group before the stretch.

HOW AND WHEN TO STRETCH

Frequency: Try to stretch every day; do each stretch 3 times per muscle.

Intensity: Light pressure, about 30-40% of max.

Duration: Hold each stretch for 60 seconds: <u>Not more than 90 seconds.</u>

If you are unable to stretch on a daily basis, a pre- and post-workout stretch is necessary. After a warm-up, but before the workout, do each of the 12 stretches twice, and after the workout one more time, for a total of three reps for each stretch.

Stretch Routine
(Follow the stretches in sequence)

1) Gastrocnemius Stretch

- Keep the front knee slightly bent and the back knee straight with the heel down.
- Lean forward from the hips.
- Repeat with the other leg.

2) Soleus Stretch

- Keep both knees slightly bent.
- Lean forward from the hips.
- Keep your heels on the floor.
- Repeat with the other leg.

 Glute Stretch

- Your right foot should be placed against the wall so that the right knee is as close to 90 degrees as is comfortable.
- Place your left ankle just past the right knee.
- Make sure the pelvis/hip area is not floating in the air; keep it as close to the floor as possible.
- Keep your shoulders on the floor.
- Repeat on the other side.

 Hamstring Stretch

- Best performed on a corner wall so that one leg is up and the other straight.
- Keep the knee of your leg on the wall slightly bent (do not force straight).
- Keep your hips and pelvis square.
- If you feel a pull in the pelvis/abdominal area, place a pillow under the knee of the straight leg.
- Repeat with the other leg.

 Groin Stretch

- Make sure both upper and lower back are flat against the wall.
- Keep shoulders level and square.
- Do not force the groin muscles to be stretched.

6. Piriformis Stretch

- Try to keep shoulders and pelvis/hips on the floor.
- Place your left foot on the opposite side of the right knee.
- Gently pull your knee toward the floor with your right arm.
- Repeat on the other side.
- If you have difficulty reaching your knee, place more pillows behind the neck and shoulders.

7. Outer Leg Stretch

- Try to keep shoulders and pelvis/hips on floor.
- Bring left foot up to rest on the right knee.
- Your left thigh should be at 90 degrees to upper body.
- Gently pull your knee toward the floor with your right arm.
- Repeat on the other side.
- If you have difficulty reaching knee, place more pillows behind the neck and shoulders.

8. Hip Flexor Stretch

- Make sure both hips and pelvis are square.
- Do not let your front knee go beyond 90 degrees.
- Try to keep lower back and upper body straight.
- Repeat with other leg forward.

(Alternative for people with bad knees.)

9 Lower Back Stretch

- Keep your toes, ankles, and knees together.
- Bring your knees up until they are 90 degrees with the upper body.
- Slowly move your top shoulder back while trying to keep the knees together.
- Repeat on the other side.

10 Tricep/Rhomboids/Rear Deltoids Stretch

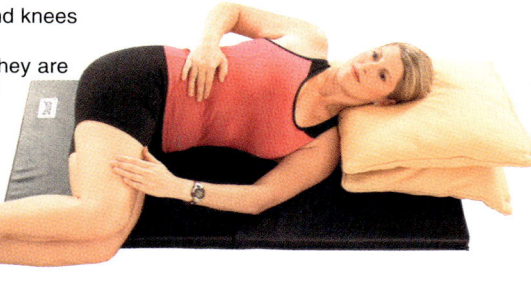

- Make sure your shoulders are square and down.
- Slowly and gently pull your arm across the front of your body.
- Try to keep the lower back and upper body straight.

11 Upper Deltoid Stretch

- Behind your back, grasp your right elbow with the left hand.
- Keep the shoulders down.
- Do not force this stretch.
- Repeat on the other side.

12 Chest/Anterior Deltoid Stretch

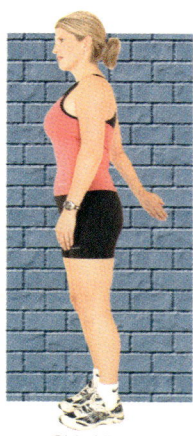

- Place a hand on the wall so that your arm is down and slightly behind your back.
- Make sure the shoulders are square and down.
- Place your feet shoulder-width apart.
- Gently twist your body away from the arm on the wall.

Side View   Back View

BARBELL EXERCISES

Shoulders

Front Press-Seated (Shoulder Press)

Muscles Worked
Deltoids, Trapezius, Triceps

1. Sit comfortably on the bench with the backrest in an upright position.
2. The bench should be placed so the bar can be lifted off the rack with minimal movement.
3. Grasp the bar with an overhand grip, slightly wider than shoulder-width apart.
4. Bring the bar to the start position so that your upper arms are parallel to the floor.
5. Set your back, then slowly press the bar overhead to full arm extension—keep your wrists locked and elbows slightly bent (do not lock your elbows). This motion should be slow and controlled throughout the exercise.
6. Pause briefly in the upper position, then slowly return the bar to the start position.

Variations:
Narrow grip (elbows forward)—increases load on the anterior deltoid/upper chest.
Wide grip (elbows out)—increases load on the anterior/medial deltoid.

- **This exercise should be avoided if there are blood pressure or lower back health problems.**
- **Do not arch your back during this exercise.**

Military Press

Muscles Worked: Deltoids, Trapezius, Triceps

START

FINISH

1. Stand upright with your feet slightly wider than shoulder-width apart and knees slightly bent.
2. Grasp the bar with an overhand grip, shoulder-width apart.
3. Bring the bar down to rest slightly on your upper chest, just in front of the shoulders.
4. Set your back, then slowly push the bar overhead to full extension (do not lock your elbows).
5. Pause briefly, then slowly return the bar to the start position.

Variations:

Narrow grip (elbows forward)—increases anterior deltoid/upper pectoralis workload.

Wide grip (elbows out)—increases anterior and medial deltoid workload.

- **Do not arch your back or neck during this exercise.**
- **Individuals with blood pressure or lower back problems should consult with their physician before beginning this exercise.**

Barbell Exercises | **25**

Upright Row

Muscles Worked
Upper Trapezius, Deltoids

 Shoulders

Note: This exercise may impinge the shoulder joint. Start with no weight and increase in small increments until a comfortable weight is achieved. **AVOID THIS EXERCISE IF YOU HAVE SHOULDER PAIN, OR STOP IF SHOULDER PAIN DEVELOPS DURING THIS EXERCISE.**

1. Stand upright with your feet comfortably apart and knees slightly bent.
2. Grasp the bar with an overhand grip slightly wider than shoulder-width apart.
3. Rest the bar on your thighs with arms fully extended.
4. Set your back, then slowly pull the bar up to your mid-chest. Keep the bar close to your body throughout the exercise. In the finish position your elbows should be higher than your wrists and above or even with your shoulders.
5. Pause briefly in the finish position, then slowly lower the bar to the start position.

Variations:
Narrower grip—increases trapezius workload.
Wider grip—increases deltoid workload.

- **Do not lift the bar higher than mid-chest as there is an increased risk of shoulder strain or injury.**
- **Do not swing or bounce the bar during the movement.**

Front Raise

Muscles Worked: Anterior Deltoid, Upper Pectorals

1. Stand upright with your feet shoulder-width apart and knees slightly bent.
2. Grasp the bar with an overhand grip, shoulder-width apart.
3. Rest the bar on your thighs.
4. Set your back, then slowly raise the bar with straight arms to shoulder level.
5. Pause briefly in the finish position, then slowly lower the bar down to the start position.

- Start with light weight to avoid excessive strain on your back.
- Excessive body swing or back arch may increase the risk of lower back strain or injury.

Barbell Exercises

Shrug

Muscles Worked: Upper Trapezius, Levator Scapula

1. Stand upright with your feet shoulder-width apart and knees slightly bent.
2. Grasp the bar with an overhand grip, slightly wider than shoulder-width apart.
3. With your arms fully extended, Set your back, then slowly "shrug" your shoulders toward your ears.
4. Pause briefly in the finish position, then slowly lower the bar to the start position.

> - **Do not roll your shoulders to the back at the top of the exercise as this may increase the risk of shoulder strain or injury.**
> - **Keep your back straight and abdominals tight throughout the movement to avoid increasing the risk of back strain.**

Push Press

Muscles Worked: Gluteus Maximus, Hamstrings, Quadriceps, Soleus, Gastrocnemius, Deltoids, Triceps, Upper Trapezius

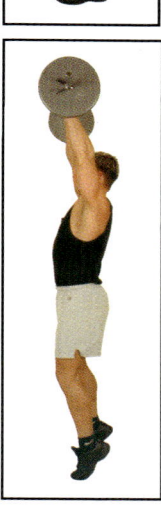

1. Stand with your feet parallel and shoulder-width apart with toes pointed out slightly.
2. Grasp the bar with an overhand grip, slightly wider than shoulder-width apart.
3. Lift the bar onto your upper chest just in front of your shoulders.
4. Bend forward at your hips, slightly bend your knees, then pause briefly.
5. Set your back, then forcefully extend your hips, knees, and elbows to push the bar 1/3 to 1/2 arm extension. Pause briefly.
6. With your hips and knees fully extended, press the bar overhead to full arm extension at the same time pushing up on to your toes.
7. Finish the movement with your elbows straight (but not locked), your head in neutral position, abdominals tight, and the bar above your head.
8. Slowly lower the bar back down to the start position resting it on your upper chest/anterior deltoids.

- Do not arch your back during this exercise.
- Avoid this exercise if you have lower back problems.
- This is an advanced exercise, so start with little or no weight on the bar until the technique has been mastered.

Bench Press

Muscles Worked: Pectoralis Major, Triceps, Anterior Deltoid

Chest

START

FINISH

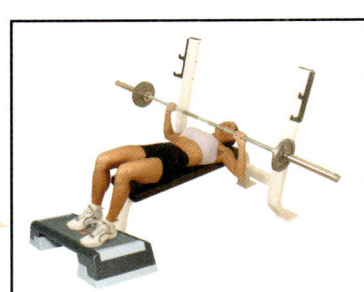

1. Lie flat on the bench with feet flat on the floor or supported on a step. Your back, buttocks, and shoulders must be in contact with the bench. (Adjust the height of the foot support to prevent your back from arching.)
2. Grasp the bar with an overhand closed grip wide enough so your forearms are perpendicular to your upper arms.
3. Move the bar off the supports (a spotter is recommended)—your arms should be fully extended and your wrists directly above your elbows.
4. Contract your abdominals and slowly lower the bar to mid-chest until your upper arms are parallel to the floor.
5. Pause briefly in the finish position, then slowly push the bar up to the start position, fully extending your elbows.

- **To avoid increasing lower back strain, do not arch the back.**
- **Do not bounce the bar off your chest.**

Bench Press- Narrow Grip

Muscles Worked: Triceps, Pectoralis Muscle

Chest

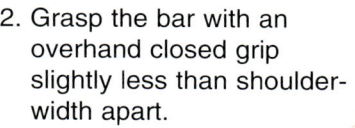
START

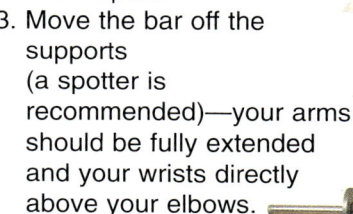
FINISH

1. Lie flat on the bench with feet flat on the floor or supported on a step. Your back, buttocks, and shoulders must be in contact with the bench.
2. Grasp the bar with an overhand closed grip slightly less than shoulder-width apart.
3. Move the bar off the supports (a spotter is recommended)—your arms should be fully extended and your wrists directly above your elbows.
4. Contract your abdominals and slowly lower the bar toward your mid-chest until your upper arms are parallel with the floor.
5. Pause briefly in the finish position, then slowly push the bar up to the start position, fully extending your elbows.

Variations:

Tight elbows—elbows at your sides during the exercise will increase the load on your anterior deltoids.

Elbows out—increases the load on your triceps.

- **To avoid increasing lower back strain, do not arch the back.**
- **Do not bounce the bar off your chest.**

Barbell Exercises | **31**

Incline Bench Press

Muscles Worked

Upper Pectorals, Anterior Deltoids, Triceps

Chest

1. Set the bench to a 30-degree incline.
2. Lie on the bench so your head is directly below the bar. Your feet should be a comfortable width apart and flat on the floor. A spotter is recommended.
3. Grasp the bar with an overhand closed grip, with your hands slightly wider than shoulder-width apart.
4. Straighten your arms to remove the bar from the rack.

5. Start by contracting your abdominals and slowly lowering the bar to your upper chest region until your upper arms are close to parallel with the floor.
6. Pause briefly in the finish position, then slowly push the bar overhead to the start position, fully extending your arms.

- **Individuals with increased shoulder flexibility may be able to lower the bar farther down.**
- **If you lack shoulder flexibility, lower the bar only until your upper arms are parallel with the floor.**
- **Do not bounce the bar off your chest.**

Pullover

Muscles Worked: Pectoralis Major, Latissimus Dorsi

Chest

1. Lie down on a bench with your feet flat on the floor or supported on the step to prevent your back from arching.
2. Grasp the bar with an overhand grip, with your hands shoulder-width apart.
3. Push the bar overhead, maintaining a slight bend in your elbows.
4. Contract your abdominals and slowly lower the bar behind your head, keeping your arms straight.
5. Pause briefly in the finish position, then slowly push the bar back up to the start position.

- To avoid increasing strain on the back and shoulders, start with a light weight.
- Do not arch your back during the exercise.
- Use a foot lift if needed to keep your back flat on the bench during the exercise.

Bent-Over Row

Muscles Worked
Latissimus Dorsi, Teres Major, Middle Trapezius, Rhomboids, Biceps, Posterior Deltoid

START — *FINISH*

1. Grasp the bar with an overhand grip, slightly wider than shoulder-width apart.
2. Bend forward at the hips until your upper body is at a 45-degree angle and your arms are fully extended. Maintain a slight bend in the knees.
3. Contract your abdominals, keep your head in a neutral position, squeeze your shoulder blades together, and slowly pull the bar to your lower chest.
4. Pause briefly in the finish position, then slowly lower the bar, returning to the start position.

- **Keep your back straight or slightly arched throughout the exercise to avoid increasing lower back strain.**

Two Arm T-Bar Row

Muscles Worked

Latissimus Dorsi, Posterior Deltoid, Middle Trapezius, Rhomboids

START

FINISH

1. Place a weight plate on one end of the bar. Place the other end of the bar into a corner to avoid movement.
2. Straddle the bar with your knees slightly bent, back straight, and the upper body at a 45-degree angle.
3. Grip the bar with both hands just below the weight plate.
4. With your arms fully extended, contract your abdominals and slowly pull the bar up to your chest.
5 Pause briefly, then slowly lower the bar back to the start position.

- **Keep your abdominals contracted, back straight, and head in neutral position throughout this exercise to avoid increasing strain on the lower back.**

Barbell Exercises | **35**

One Arm T-Bar Row

Muscles Worked
Latissimus Dorsi, Posterior Deltoid, Middle Trapezius, Rhomboids, Biceps

START   FINISH

1. Place a weight plate on one end of the bar. Place the other end of the bar into a corner to avoid movement.
2. Straddle the bar with your knees slightly bent, back straight, and the upper body at a 45-degree angle.
3. Grip the bar with one hand using an overhand grip, just below the weight plate. Place your other arm on your knee for support. Keep your head in neutral position.
4. With your arm fully extended, contract your abdominals and pull the bar up to your chest.
5. Pause briefly in the finish position, then slowly lower the bar back to the start position.

- Keep your back straight and flat, knees slightly flexed, abdominals contracted, and your head in neutral position throughout this exercise to avoid increasing back strain.

Standing Bicep Curl

Muscles Worked
Bicep Brachii, Brachialis, Brachioradialis

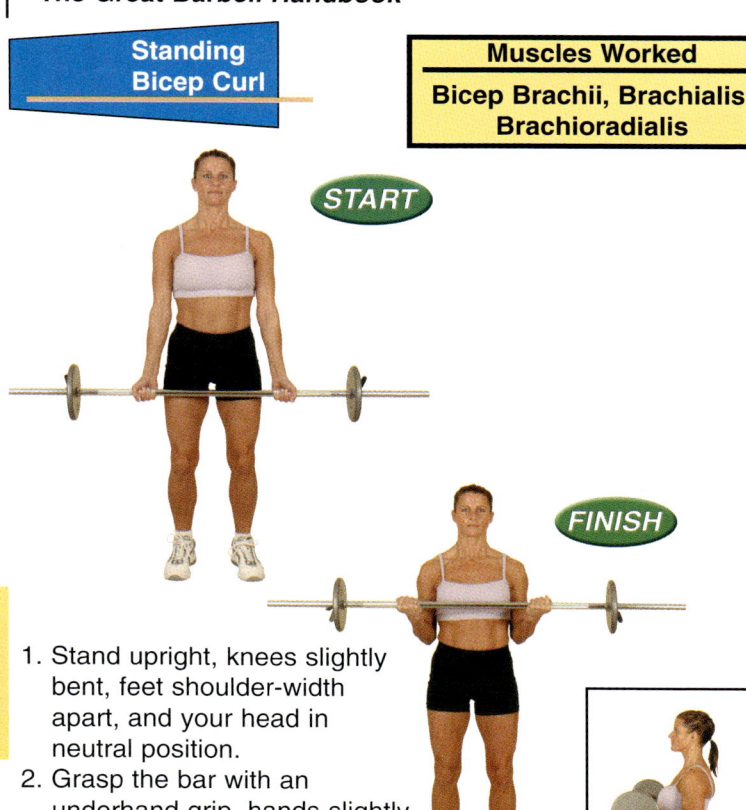

1. Stand upright, knees slightly bent, feet shoulder-width apart, and your head in neutral position.
2. Grasp the bar with an underhand grip, hands slightly wider than shoulder-width apart.
3. Rest the bar on your thighs with your arms fully extended.
4. Set your back, then slowly bend your elbows to curl the bar toward your shoulders.
5. Pause briefly in the finish position, then slowly lower the bar to the start position, fully extending your arms.

Variations:
Narrow grip—increases focus on the outer bicep.
Wide grip—increases focus on the inner bicep.
To prevent swinging the arms or arching your back, this exercise can be done with your back against a wall.

- **Do not arch your back or swing your arms during this exercise.**
- **If you need to arch your back during the exercise, use a lighter weight.**

Barbell Exercises

Bicep Curl - E-Z Kurl Bar

Muscles Worked
Brachialis, Bicep Brachii, Brachioradialis

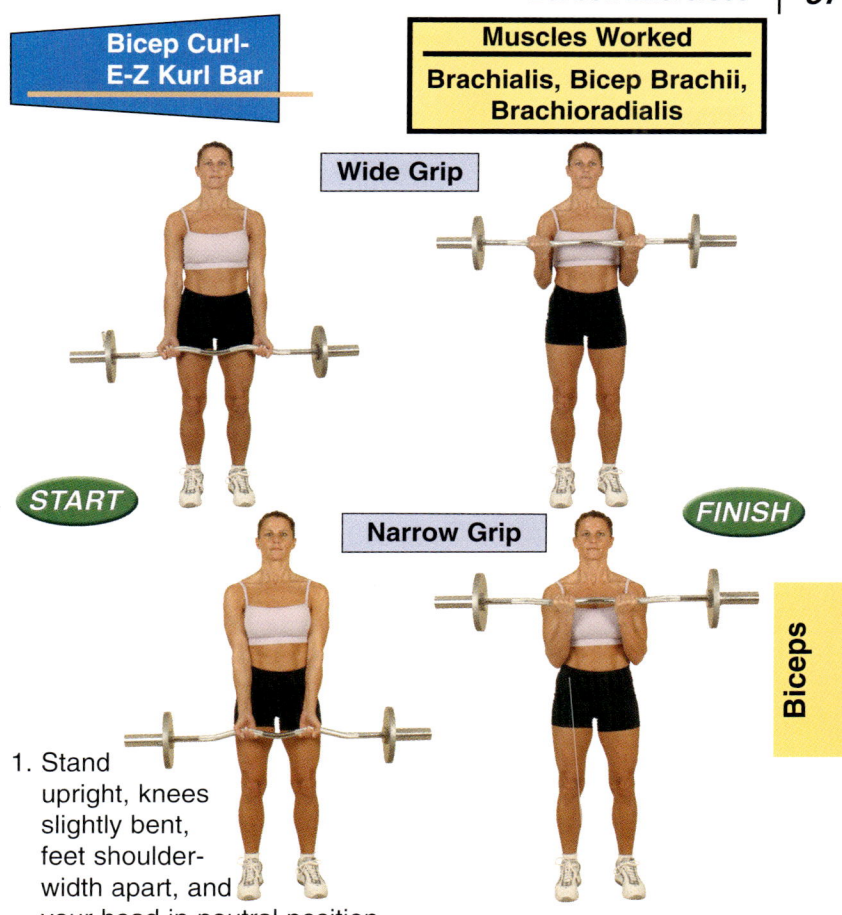

Biceps

1. Stand upright, knees slightly bent, feet shoulder-width apart, and your head in neutral position.
2. Grasp the bar with an underhand grip, shoulder-width apart.
3. Rest the bar on your thighs with your arms fully extended.
4. Contract your abdominals and slowly curl the bar toward your shoulders. Keep your elbows stationary throughout the exercise.
5. Pause briefly in the finish position, then slowly lower the bar to the start position, fully extending your arms.

Variations:
Narrow grip—increased focus on the outer bicep and brachialis.
Wide grip—increased focus on the inner bicep.
This exercise can be done against a wall to avoid swinging your arms or arching your back.

- **The E-Z Kurl bar hits the bicep from different angles but does increase wrist strain, so start with a light weight.**
- **If you need to swing your arms or arch your back, use a lighter weight.**

Seated Isolation Curl

Muscles Worked: Bicep Brachii, Brachioradialis, Brachialis

Biceps

1. Sit on the end of the bench with your feet spread slightly wider than shoulder-width apart.
2. Lean forward, straighten your arms, and rest your elbows on the inner thighs, about 2-4 inches above your knees.
3. Grasp the bar with an underhand grip, placing your hands about 12 inches apart.
4. Curl the bar up until your forearms touch your biceps. Keep your elbows fixed and motionless throughout the exercise.
5. Pause briefly in the finish position, then slowly lower the bar back to the start position, fully extending your arms.

Variations:
E-Z Kurl Bar—increases brachioradialis loading.
Narrow grip—increases the load on the outer bicep.
Wide grip—increases the load on the inner bicep.

- **Keep your elbows tight to your knees throughout this exercise to avoid increasing the stress on your lower back.**
- **Keep your head in neutral position.**

Preacher Curl-E-Z Kurl Bar

Muscles Worked

Brachialis, Biceps Brachii, Brachioradialis

1. Sit on the preacher bench with your upper arms resting on the pad.
2. Grasp the bar with an underhand grip, about shoulder-width apart, and your arms fully extended. Tighten your abdominals and set your back.
3. Slowly curl the bar up to the front of your shoulders while keeping your upper arms still.
4. Pause briefly in the finish position, then slowly lower the bar back to the start position.

Variations:
Narrow grip—increases load on the outer bicep.
Wide grip—increases load on the inner bicep.
Straight bar—increases bicep load.

> • Start with a light weight due to increased strain on your elbows when the arm is in the fully extended position.

Lying Triceps Extension

Muscles Worked: Triceps

START

FINISH

1. Lie flat on the bench with feet flat on the floor or supported on the step and your back, buttocks, and shoulders touching the bench.
2. Grasp the bar with an overhand closed grip, with your hands about 12 inches apart.
3. Straighten your arms overhead (a spotter is recommended).
4. Contract your abdominals and bend your elbows while slowly lowering the bar behind your head. Keep your elbows fixed and motionless throughout the exercise.
5. Pause briefly in the finish position, then slowly push the bar up to the start position.

Variations:

Forehead—slowly lowering the bar to your forehead increases the load on the inner and outer triceps, whereas lowering the bar behind your head increases the load on the long head of the triceps.

Floor—this exercise can also be done lying on the floor.
Caution: This exercise must be done slowly.

- **To avoid increasing back strain, do not arch your back, and start with a light weight until the technique is mastered.**

Seated Triceps Extension

Muscles Worked: Triceps

START — FINISH

1. Sit on a flat bench with your legs comfortably apart and your feet flat on the floor.
2. Grasp an E-Z Kurl bar in an overhand grip with your hands 12 inches apart. To get into the start position, lift the bar overhead.
3. Slowly lower the bar behind your head, keeping your upper arms straight, only bending at the elbow.
4. Keep your elbows pointing straight ahead, parallel and fixed during the entire exercise.
5. Pause briefly in the finish position, then slowly straighten your arms overhead to the start position.

Variation:
This exercise can be done with the tricep bar or straight bar.

- **To avoid increasing lower back strain, keep your abdominals tight and your back straight throughout the exercise.**
- **Do not arch your back.**
- **If available, use the bench with a back support for this exercise.**

Standing Overhead Triceps Extension

Muscles Worked: Triceps

1. Stand upright with your knees slightly bent and your abdominals contracted.
2. Grasp the bar with an overhand closed grip (straight bar) or neutral grip (Tricep Bar), with your hands 6-12 inches apart.
3. Lift the bar straight overhead, maintaining a slight bend at the elbows.
4. Keep your upper arms stiff and straight up.
5. Bending at the elbows, slowly lower the bar behind your head.
6. Keep your elbows pointed straight up, parallel and fixed during the entire exercise.
7. Pause briefly in the finish position, then slowly push the bar up to the start position.

- To avoid increasing lower back strain, tighten the abdominals and do not arch the back.
- A spotter is encouraged for any overhead lifts.

Barbell Exercises | **43**

Barbell Kickback

Muscles Worked
Triceps

1. Stand with the bar on the floor behind you. Squat down, grasping the bar with an overhand grip, hands about shoulder-width apart.
2. Slowly return to a standing position so that the bar is touching your rear thighs.
3. Lean forward while bending your knees slightly and keeping your upper arms fixed at your sides, bending them only at the elbows. Maintain tight abdominals, flat back, and your head in a neutral alignment or slightly arched.
4. The bar is now directly behind your knees and you are in the start position.
5. Slowly straighten your arms, keeping your upper arms fixed. The only point of movement is at the elbows.
6. Pause briefly in the finish position, then slowly return the bar back to the start position.

- **Movement must take place from the elbows to isolate the triceps.**
- **Do not swing the arms or body during the exercise.**

Reverse Grip Bench Press

Muscles Worked: Triceps, Anterior Deltoid

Triceps

1. Lie flat on the bench with your feet flat on the floor or supported on the step. Your back, buttocks, and shoulders must be in contact with the bench.
2. Grasp the bar with an underhand (reverse) grip and hands slightly less than shoulder-width apart.
3. Move the bar off the supports (a spotter is recommended). To get into the start position, your arms should be fully extended.
4. Contract your abdominals and slowly lower the bar to your mid-chest until your upper arms are parallel with the floor. To fully isolate the triceps, your elbows must be at your sides during the movement.
5. Pause briefly in the finish position, then slowly push the bar up until your elbows are fully extended.

- **To avoid increasing lower back strain, do not arch your back during the exercise.**
- **Do not bounce the bar off your chest.**

Reverse Curl

Muscles Worked
Wrist Extensors, Brachioradialis, Brachialis, Biceps Brachii

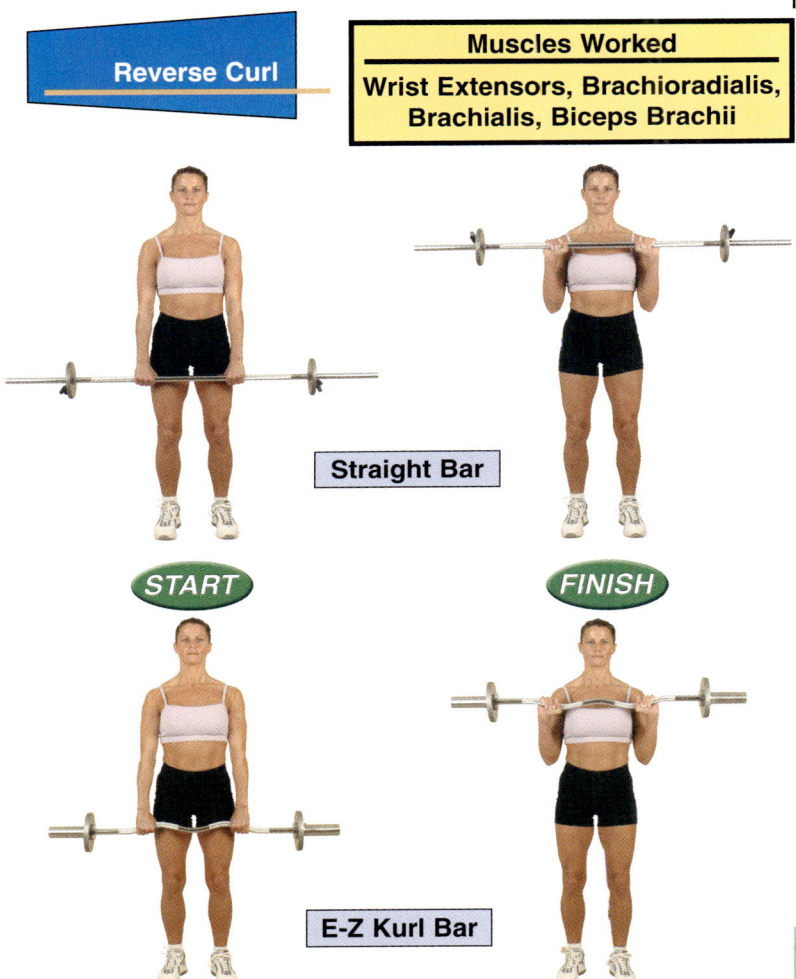

Straight Bar

START FINISH

E-Z Kurl Bar

1. Grasp the bar with an overhand grip, shoulder-width apart.
2. Stand upright with feet comfortably apart, knees bent slightly, and your arms fully extended at your sides.
3. Curl the bar up, keeping your upper arms fixed, and bending at the elbows. Continue until the bar reaches about 4-6 inches in front of your chest and shoulders.
4. Pause briefly in the finish position, then slowly lower the bar to the start position.

Variation:
Narrow grip—increases load on the brachioradialis.

- **Do not swing your arms or arch your back during the exercise.**

Wrist Curl-Bench

Muscles Worked: Wrist and Finger Flexors

1. Grasp the bar with an underhand grip, with your hands 4-6 inches apart.
2. Sit on a flat bench and lean forward to rest your forearms on the bench.
3. Extend your wrist and fingers beyond the edge of the bench.
4. Get into the start position by slowly letting the weight of the bar extend your wrists and fingers until the bar is resting in your fingertips.
5. Curl your fingers and wrists up towards your forearms.
6. Pause briefly at the end of the range of motion, then slowly lower the bar back to the start position.

Barbell Exercises

Reverse Wrist Curl-Bench

Muscles Worked

Wrist and Finger Extensors

START

FINISH

1. Grasp the bar with an overhand grip, with your hands about 4-6 inches apart.
2. Sit on the bench with your feet spread wider than shoulder-width apart.
3. To get into the start position, lean forward and rest your forearms on the bench, extend your wrists beyond the end of the bench and passively flex your wrists, letting the weight of the bar pull your hands down.
4. Lift the bar, extending your wrists back without moving your arms or elbows.
5. Pause briefly in the finish position, then slowly lower the bar to the start position.

Forearms

Wrist Curl-Thighs

Muscles Worked: Wrist and Finger Flexors

START

FINISH

1. Grasp the bar with an underhand grip, with your hands 4-6 inches apart.
2. Sit on the end of the bench with your feet 10 inches apart, toes pointed straight ahead, and legs parallel.
3. Lean forward and rest your forearms on your thighs with your wrists out beyond your knees.
4. Get into the start position by passively extending your wrists and fingers as far as possible, letting the weight of the bar pull your hands down.
5. Curl the bar up toward your forearms while keeping your elbows and arms in contact with your thighs throughout the exercise.
6. Pause briefly in the finish position, then slowly lower the bar back to the start position.

Barbell Exercises | **49**

Reverse Wrist Curl-Thighs

Muscles Worked
Wrist and Finger Extensors

1. Sit on the end of the bench with your feet approximately 10 inches apart.
2. Grasp the bar with an overhand grip, your hands 8-12 inches apart.
3. To get into the start position, lean forward and rest your forearms on your thighs. Place your wrists beyond your knees.
4. Passively flex your wrists as far as possible, letting the weight of the bar pull your hands down.
5. Extend your wrists back, bringing the bar up. Keep your arms and elbows in place throughout the motion.
6. Pause briefly in the finish position, then slowly lower the bar to the start position.

Forearms

Behind-The-Back Wrist Curl

Muscles Worked: Wrist and Finger Flexors

1. Stand upright with your feet shoulder-width apart.
2. Grasp the bar behind your back. Your hands are shoulder-width apart with an overhand grip.
3. In the start position your wrists are straight, hands open with the bar resting in your curled fingertips.
4. Contract the abdominals, and curl your wrists up as far as possible without leaning forward or swinging your body.
5. Pause briefly in the finish position, then slowly lower the bar to the start position.

Front Squat

Muscles Worked
Gluteus Maximus, Quadriceps, Hamstrings

1. Grasp the bar with either of the grips below. Place the bar on the upper chest and shoulders (will vary a little with the grip selected).
2. Place your feet shoulder-width apart with your toes slightly pointed out.
3. Inhale, set your back, then slowly squat down, bending at the hips and knees. Keep your heels on the floor, knees over your toes, back flat, and your eyes focused ahead.
4. Slowly descend until your thighs are parallel with the floor.
5. Pause briefly in the finish position, then exhale and slowly straighten your hips and knees to return to the upright start position.

Variations (Grip):

Crossed—arms are bent and crossed in front of chest. Open grip with the hands on top of the bar.

Parallel—closed grip, shoulder width apart. Upper arms are close to parallel with the floor and elbows held high.

- Do not let your knees travel in front of your toes during this exercise.
- Keep your head up, chest out, and back flat.
- Start with little or no weight until the technique has been mastered.

High Bar Back Squat

Muscles Worked: Quadriceps, Gluteus Maximus, Hamstrings

Placement of Bar

Caution: Make sure the bar is placed on the muscles below (and not on) the spinal bones at the base of the neck.

1. Set the bar height at the mid-to-upper chest level.
2. Step under the bar, carefully positioning it behind your head on the upper back and shoulder muscles, just below the spinal bones.
3. Grasp the bar with a wide overhand closed grip.
4. Lift your elbows up and set your back.
5. Straighten your knees and hips to lift the bar off the rack.
6. Step back 1-2 steps and align your feet parallel and shoulder-width apart (a slight toe-out position may be more comfortable for some individuals).
7. Inhale, set your back, then slowly squat by bending at the hips and knees. Keep your back flat, chest up and out, and head level (don't hyper-extend).
8. Keep your heels on the floor and knees over your toes.

Legs

High Bar Back Squat (continued)

9. Continue slowly lowering the bar until your thighs are close to parallel with the floor or as far as your natural range of motion will allow.
10. Pause briefly in the finish position, then exhale while slowly straightening your hips and knees to move back to the upright position.
11. Once the desired repetitions have been completed, step forward and replace the bar on the rack.

Variations:

Low bar—place the bar across the shoulders and upper back about 1-2 inches below high bar position—your grip will be wider than your shoulders (how wide you go will depend on shoulder flexibility). This is used more often by powerlifters.

- **In the beginning, this exercise should be completed with no weight or very little weight until correct technique has been mastered.**
- **Do not let your knees go in front of your toes during the exercise.**
- **Keep your head up, chest out, and back flat.**

Power Squat

Muscles Worked
Quadriceps, Adductors, Gluteals, Hamstrings

1. Set the racks so the bar is slightly below shoulder level.
2. Grasp the bar with a wide overhand grip.
3. Carefully position yourself so the bar is behind your head and resting on the upper back and shoulder muscles, just below the spinal bones.
4. Lift your elbows slightly and set your back as you straighten your hips and knees to slowly lift the bar off the rack.
5. Position yourself in the center of the squat rack.
6. Keep your back set, knees out and in-line with your toes throughout the exercise.
7. Inhale then slowly bend at your hips and knees until the thighs are almost parallel with the floor.
8. Pause briefly in the finish position, exhale, then straighten your hips and knees to slowly return to the upright start position.

- Throughout the exercise keep upright posture with a flat back and your head in neutral alignment.
- Start with little or light weight until you have mastered the technique.
- Individuals will vary in the depth of the squat, depending on flexibility. Going past the parallel position is not recommended for beginners.

Barbell Exercises | **55**

Split Squat

Muscles Worked

Gluteus Maximus, Quadriceps

Placement of Bar

Caution: Make sure the bar is placed on the muscles below (and not on) the spinal bones at the base of the neck.

1. Take an overhand closed grip with your hands wider than shoulder-width apart.
2. Carefully place the bar behind your head on the upper back and shoulder muscles, just below the spinal bones.
3. Stand upright with your feet shoulder-width apart and one leg placed 3-4 feet in front of the other.
4. Keep your upper body erect and eyes focused straight ahead throughout the exercise.
5. From the start position, inhale as you slowly bend your front knee, lowering your body until your front thigh is parallel to the floor and the back knee is close to the floor.
6. Do not let your front knee go in front of your toes, or the back knee touch the floor.
7. Pause briefly, then exhale as you straighten your legs to return to the start position.

- **Do not let your front knee travel beyond your toes at any time during the exercise.**

Legs

Lunge

Muscles Worked: Gluteus Maximus, Hamstrings, Quadriceps

1. Stand upright with your feet shoulder-width apart.
2. Grip the bar using an overhand closed grip with your hands placed wider than shoulder-width apart.
3. To get into the start position, carefully put the bar behind your head, on the upper back and shoulder muscles, just below the spinal bones.
4. Inhale as you step forward with your right leg, landing with a flat foot about 3 feet in front. Keep your back upright and chest up and out.
5. Bend the front knee until your thigh is parallel to the floor and your back knee approaches the floor. Do not let your front knee go in front of your toes.
6. Pause briefly, then exhale as you push off your front leg to return to the start position.
7. Repeat alternating legs.

Variations:

A small stride increases the workload on the quadriceps of your front leg.

A large stride increases gluteal and hamstring load on your front leg.

Small Stride

- Always keep your abdominal muscles tight throughout the exercise.
- This is an advanced exercise that may create balance problems for the beginner—start without weight until the technique is mastered, or begin with the "split squat" exercise.
- Do not let your front knee go beyond your toes at any time during the exercise.

Barbell Exercises

Side Lunge

Muscles Worked
Adductors, Gluteus Maximus, Hamstrings, Quadriceps

Placement of Bar

Caution: Make sure the bar is placed on the muscles below (and not on) the spinal bones at the base of the neck.

1. Grasp the bar with a closed overhand grip, wider than shoulder-width apart.
2. Carefully place the bar behind your head on your upper back and shoulder muscles, just below the spinal bones.
3. Stand upright with your feet parallel and about 12-18 inches apart.
4. Inhale, then contract your abdominals. Using your left foot, step back and to the side, landing with a flat foot. Bend your front knee until your thigh is almost parallel to the floor.
5. Make sure your right knee never comes out past the toes. Keep your back straight, chest up and out, and eyes focused ahead.
6. Pause briefly in the finish position, then exhale as you push off, bringing your left leg back to the start position.
7. Repeat, alternating legs.

- **If balance is a problem during this exercise, begin with little or no weight.**

Step Up

Muscles Worked
Gluteus Maximus, Hamstrings, Quadriceps

1. Grasp the bar with a wide overhand grip.
2. Carefully place the bar behind your head on the upper back and shoulder muscles, just below the spinal bones.
3. Start with your feet slightly apart and parallel, about 12-18 inches in front of the step.
4. Bring your chest up and out, look straight ahead, and squeeze your shoulder blades together.
5. Step forward with your left foot, placing it entirely on top of the step—do not let your knee go in front of your toes.
6. Shift your weight to the left foot as you push off with the right foot, stepping up and planting both feet firmly on top of the step.
7. Pause briefly, then shift your weight back onto the left foot as you step backwards off the step with your right foot, planting it firmly on the floor.
8. Finish by pushing off slightly with your left foot, shifting the weight to your right to bring both feet back onto the floor.
9. Repeat, alternating left and right legs.

- **This exercise should be done without additional weight or with a spotter until balance and technique are mastered.**

Barbell Exercises

Conventional Deadlift

Muscles Worked
Gluteus Maximus, Hamstrings, Quadriceps, Erector Spinae

1. Stand facing the bar with your feet shoulder-width apart and toes slightly pointed out.
2. Bend forward from the hips with your knees bent and keeping your back as straight as possible.
3. With your arms fully extended, grasp the bar with an overhand or alternated grip, slightly wider than shoulder-width apart.
4. In the start position your back should be flat, head in a neutral or slightly arched position, with your shoulders slightly in front of the bar.
5. Set your back, then slowly lift the bar off the floor by straightening your hips and knees.
6. Keep your arms fully extended and the bar close to your body throughout the movement.
7. Exhale as the bar passes your knees, move your hips forward, gently touching the bar against your thighs.
8. When you are fully upright, stick your chest up and out and hold for 2-3 seconds.
9. Slowly bend your hips and knees to lower the bar back to the floor. Keep your back straight and do not lean forward during the movement.

- **Individuals with lower back problems should avoid this exercise.**
- **Use light weight to start until good technique has been developed.**
- **This is an advanced exercise and beginners should start with little or no weight until the technique is mastered.**

Legs

Sumo Deadlift

Muscles Worked

Erector Spinae, Quadriceps, Adductors, Hamstrings, Gluteus Muscles

1. To get into the start position, stand facing the bar with your feet wider than shoulder-width apart and toes pointing out.
2. Keeping your back straight, squat down, bending your knees until your thighs are almost parallel to the floor.
3. Place you arms between your knees and grasp the bar with arms fully extended, using an overhand or alternated grip.
4. Inhale, set your back, then slowly stand upright by straightening your hips and knees at the same time.
5. Once in the upright position, exhale and pause for 2-3 seconds.
6. Then slowly lower the bar back to the start position by bending at the hips and knees.

Note:
This exercise puts more emphasis on the quadriceps and adductors due to the more upright start position.

- **Start with light weight and develop good technique.**
- **Keep your back straight or slightly arched, chest up and out, shoulder blades squeezed together, and your head in neutral alignment throughout the exercise.**

Seated Calf Raise

Muscles Worked: Soleus

START

FINISH

1. Sit on the bench with your back straight.
2. Grasp the bar with an overhand, comfortable grip and place the bar across your thighs. If you are uncomfortable resting the bar on your thighs, place a towel over your thighs to pad them.
3. Your heels should be hanging over the edge of the step, with your toes and the balls of your feet on the step.
4. Get into the start position by slowly lowering your heels toward the floor until they are at their lowest position.
5. S lowly raise your heels by pushing the balls of your feet into the step. Continue until you are as high as possible.
6. Pause briefly in the finish position, then slowly lower your heels to the start position.

Variation:
This exercise can be done initially without weight.

- **Start with a light weight since this exercise isolates the soleus.**

Other products by
Productive Fitness Products Inc.

More than a <u>one-year personal fitness diary</u>, *The Ultimate Weight Training Journal* discusses basic nutrition, aerobics, and strength training. But best of all, this book shows you how these three tools can best be used in attaining a better physique, better health, and more strength.

One Year of Training Log pages based on 3-4 workouts per week

288 pages

The Ultimate Weight Training Journal
Canada $18.95
U.S. $14.95

If you own or are thinking about purchasing a home gym, *The Great Home Gym Handbook* will guide you through all the steps of setting up your own program, which exercises to do, the proper exercise technique, and how to maintain your home gym. In addition, it discusses how to stretch, how to stay motivated, the importance of aerobic training, and safety tips. This book is written in a clear and concise manner, with step-by-step instructions and photos for all exercises.

64 pages

The Great Home Gym Handbook
Canada $10.95
U.S. $ 8.95

If you have stretch tubing at home or are thinking about purchasing some, *The Great Stretch Tubing Handbook* is a must. This little book has all the different stretch tubing exercises you need for working your whole body. In addition, it discusses how to make and use a door attachment, and includes a sample routine and a rotator cuff section. It also includes safety tips and muscle diagrams. This book is written in a clear and concise manner, with step-by-step instructions and photos for all exercises.

64 pages

The Great Stretch Tubing Handbook
Canada $10.95
U.S. $ 8.95

If you own a body ball or are thinking about purchasing one, *The Great Body Ball Handbook* is a must. This little book has all the different ball exercises you need for working your whole body. In addition, it discusses how to choose the correct ball size, proper ball inflation, and includes a sample routine. It also includes safety tips and muscle diagrams. This book is written in a clear and concise manner, with step-by-step instructions and photos for all exercises.

64 pages

The Great Body Ball Handbook
Canada $10.95
U.S. $ 8.95

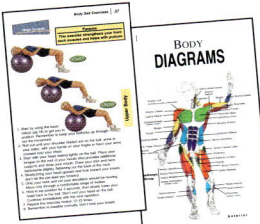

If you are an athlete in training or in good physical condition, *The Great Medicine Ball Handbook* is a must. This little book has all the different medicine ball exercises you need for working your whole body. In addition, it discusses rotator cuff exercises and gives a sample routine. It also includes safety tips and muscle diagrams. This book is written in a clear and concise manner, with step-by-step instructions and photos for all exercises.

64 pages

The Great Medicine Ball Handbook
Canada $10.95
U.S. $ 8.95

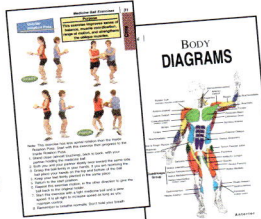

If you have a set of dumbbells at home or you are thinking about purchasing some, *The Great Dumbbell Handbook* is a must. This little book has all the different dumbbell exercises you need for working your whole body. In addition, it discusses how to set up a program, how to set up your own mini-gym, how to stretch, how to stay motivated, and includes safety tips. This book is written in a clear and concise manner, with step-by-step instructions and photos for all exercises.

64 pages

The Great Dumbbell Handbook
Canada $10.95
U.S. $ 8.95

If you own barbells, or are thinking about purchasing some, *The Great Barbell Handbook* will guide you through all the steps of setting up your own program, which exercises to do, and the proper exercise techniques. In addition, it discusses how to stretch, how to stay motivated, the importance of aerobic training, and safety tips. This book is written in a clear and concise manner, with step-by-step instructions and photos for all exercises.

64 pages

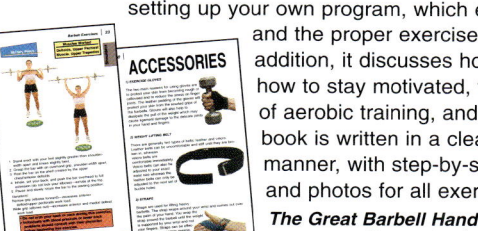

The Great Barbell Handbook
Canada $10.95
U.S. $ 8.95

Body Ball Training Poster Pack
- Four Full-Color 12" x 18" Posters -

Four posters sold as a set only

Body Ball Training Poster Pack

<u>Laminated</u>
- Canada $29.95
- US $22.95

• These four full-color, laminated posters will make your ball workouts more effective by allowing you to quickly identify proper exercise form and technique.

Dumbbell Training Poster Pack
- Four Full-Color 12" x 18" Posters -

Dumbbell Training Poster Pack

<u>Laminated</u>
- Canada $29.95
- US $22.95

• These four full-color posters will make your dumbbell workouts more effective by allowing you to quickly identify proper exercise form and technique.

Stretch Tubing Training Poster Pack
- Five Full-Color 12" x 18" Posters -

Stretch Tubing Poster Pack

<u>Laminated</u>
- Canada $29.95
- US $22.95

• These five full-color, laminated posters will make your stretch tubing workout more effective by allowing you to quickly identify proper exercise form and technique.